Previous Praise for Danielle (
Delinquent Palaces

Everything is alive and fully charged in Chapman's poetry of ardor and loss, survival and renewal as she revels in the music of language — the fruitiness of vowels, the clash of consonants, the swoon of rhyme. Incisive, bemused, and impassioned, Chapman gives strong and lucid voice to the rapture of existence and the mysteries of consciousness.

Donna Seaman, *Booklist*, Starred Review

Danielle Chapman's poetry is brilliant, mysterious, and impetuous in its quest for intensity. Like Gerard Manley Hopkins, she knows the secret to charging the world with grandeur, with words and their music; like his windhover, her words buckle in two senses: both secured and "halted in a breakbeat."

Ange Mlinko

Delinquent Palaces is one of those rare things, a first book of an already developed, master poet. The one who looks out from the "yard that has been left untended / by any hand but the that of God." And the name of that yard is music.

Ilya Kaminsky

For Chapman, love is a matter of piercing, irreverent enchantments and chastening tragedies, a symbol of grace and an inevitable source of pain. The poems in *Delinquent Palaces* show this again and again, and they suggest what poetry offers its readers, not just in National Poetry Month but the whole year-round: a reminder that, if we look, we will see a world bathed in beauty and terror, "the fire hydrants redder / than berries of blood on islands of thorn."

Anthony Domestico, *Commonweal*

This is a first book of great breadth, means, and detail. Chapman's landscapes — mostly American, all over America — are familiar and strange, animated by startling metaphor.

Daisy Fried, *On the Seawall*

Previous Praise for *Holler: A Poet Among Patriots*

There's no opportunism here, no pandering to the political side to which she belongs, no sacrificing of one's "problematic" family in order to absolve oneself. What Chapman has done with this book is much riskier, and more interesting, and more beautiful.

Kate Lucky, *Commonweal*

[A] dramatic, frank, witty, and intellectually lush family memoir. ... [Chapman] brings her ancestors to vivid, fully human life with ringing details and compassionate insights, recounting the splintery oddities of her youth in a world right out of Flannery O'Connor. Chapman is a sure-fire storyteller as she also deploys her poet's gifts for ravishing language and resonant metaphors in this thoughtfully intricate tale of loss, love, and moral quandaries in which the verdant land itself is a vital presence.

Donna Seaman, *Booklist*, starred review

Chapman's richly lyrical yet incisive voice never falters. ... This is what the memoir achieves: an angle of repose, an integration of opposites, an acceptance of paradox. Just as those who loved her contained both shadow and light, so Chapman herself is rich with contradictions. She tells a story that in a way belongs to all of us. We are simultaneously unforgivable and worthy of the deepest compassion. We are failures, and yet our efforts sometimes salvage beauty from the ruins.

Elizabeth Genovise, *Plough*

Holler traces out the strands of self, place, and history that bind us to any past we claim or disclaim, that live on in our pride and regret, our nerves and our senses.

Marilynne Robinson

With blazing lyric intensity, [Chapman's] story builds to a conclusion of mythic power and surprise made real in every phrase of her phosphorescent prose. An astonishment. A lesson in being human.

Rosanna Warren

Danielle Chapman's *Holler* is a magical and rare species of a book. ... I am moved by the grace this book seeks and the textured moments it evokes.

Major Jackson

In a time when so many offer lip-service instead of actual reckoning, Chapman [is] ... full of character, full of refusal to speak in platitudes, full of personality and heart, brimming with the kind of verbal music that makes emotion come alive for the reader almost viscerally (indeed, few can write a prose as musical and precise as Chapman's). *Holler* is stunning book.

Ilya Kaminsky

Holler is exquisite and moving, an excavation of personal history and national mythologies, and Danielle Chapman's complex and sensitive approach offers a brave and insightful path forward as we confront the past.

Philip Klay

Chapman has broken into the past without prejudice. This is new.

Fanny Howe

Boxed
Juice

Boxed
Juice Danielle
Chapman

UNBOUND EDITION PRESS

Atlanta

FIRST EDITION

Printed in the United States of America

LIBRARY OF CONGRESS RECORD

Name: Chapman, Danielle, 1976 — author.
Title: Boxed Juice / Danielle Chapman.
Edition: First edition.
Published: Atlanta : Unbound Edition Press, 2024.

LCCN: 2023934946
LCCN Permalink: https://lccn.loc.gov/2023934946
ISBN: 979-8-9870199-4-8 (fine softcover)

Designed by Eleanor Safe and Joseph Floresca
Printed by Bookmobile, Minneapolis, MN
Distributed by Itasca Books

23456789

Unbound Edition Press
1270 Caroline Street, Suite D120
Box 448
Atlanta, GA 30307

The Unbound Edition Press logo and name are
registered trademarks of Unbound Edition LLC.

PERMANENT

For Christian, Eliza, and Fiona

And I was alive in the blizzard of the blossoming pear,
Myself I stood in the storm of the bird-cherry tree.

OSIP MANDELSTAM

Contents

I.

Boxed
Juice

Foreword

In "The Poem" at the opening of this book, Danielle Chapman calls the enduring force of poetry, its power through suffering, "the wild arrowing of words toward their fates." With a writer as true as Chapman, single phrases often reveal fundamental stakes, and in fact this poet is fascinated by both wildness and fate, their competing claims on us, and their surprising conjunctions. The image of "wild arrowing" also suggests what Chapman's poems *feel like*, their simultaneous senses of unpredictability and inevitability, romance and disillusionment, linguistic largesse and last-ditch directness, precision and danger. It's the ability to render such different tones, emotions, and beliefs that gives *Boxed Juice* its depth and dimension and makes Danielle Chapman so important to poetry right now.

At the heart of the book lies the poet's attempt to hold herself and her family together during her husband's struggle with near-fatal cancer. For all its elegance, this remains a work pitched against despair, an act of survival. The resources she summons for the task — intensity, concision, ironic humor, verbal fire, and sheer nerve, to name a few — are those of the lyric poet. But these poems show a quality I associate with Shakespeare's plays because Chapman has something rare, an original vision of being, what Dr. Johnson had in mind when he wrote, "Shakespeare's plays are not in the rigorous and critical sense either tragedies or comedies, but compositions of a distinct kind; exhibiting the real state of sublunary nature, which partakes of good and evil, joy and sorrow ... "

You can find the "the real state of sublunary nature" on every page of *Boxed Juice*. A tragic-comic sensibility informs "Putting One on at Maxim's," for example, in which the poet acts as a hostess for a humorous literary event while "elsewhere in the city/Nurses fed her husband a cocktail of Thalidomide." Reading these poems often means entertaining very different feelings simultaneously. In "Friday Migraine," the agony described verges toward the ecstatic even as it remains believably agonizing. The girl in "Catch-All" experiences something similar when she tells her mother that the nettles she gripped "stung me into seeing." Chapman trusts what remains through both bliss and pain.

Consider the unsentimental praise with which she ends "Unspeakable":

> Do you see
> the dogwood's sensitivity —
> all these deep red crepe cups
> candelabraed up

from Mrs. Abraham Malherbe's
lichen-lepered tree?
They skewer the sky
with the austere

ash-pointed spurs
of why they're here
no matter where they wish,
or if they wish, to be.

Like those dogwood blossoms, Danielle Chapman's poems
are tenacious and surprising, wild and fated, there with us for
the bad as well as the good. No matter where we may wish to
be, they meet us in the world where we are.

Peter Campion

The Poem

You know it hadn't a drop to do with love
except that if I showed you how
salt boiled on each winding stair
back into that Baudelairean
cellar eaved in velvet,
your ear might love mine more for it.

Surely I'd gone partly mad
but can it have been madness if it yielded
a sound like a fruit spasming its pit
out into a stellar void that read
the shaggy, wet ridge of its cleaved heart
as the one sane absolute?

Surely I sought strangeness when
I ought to have sought repetition, yet
married and tired, tired to the marrow,
the wild arrowing of words toward their fates
still unseizures sweet Nadezhdas
into the *wyrd* we've shared.

I.

Leaving Boston

Burgundy geometries of waiting chairs recede
and magazines flap open behind us

as we smack through overpasses
like waves of a whopping headache
and rowers in late sun
dip trim oars into the Charles in unison.

Ibrutinib. Ibrutinib.

There is a discipline, a sport to hope:
to pray for prayers that break the surface whether

you're better or (*please Jesus never*)
worse.

Advent

I hear the refrigerator's hum
turn over, the seltzer's
minareting spores

while downstairs the girls direct
a play in which a scored balloon
named Lily Amulet is lain
in her bassinet against
the stratagems of her evil brother,
Stinky Butt, embodied
by an orchid —

yet no argument, nothing but
soft rips of gift wrap and unmasked
tape as they negotiate
the haying of Amulet's
crèche.

No crisis, accelerating
into victorious survival, clocked
by revolving
arrivals at the hospital.

Just mistletoe and frankincense,
blue lights and candy canes blinking
red over a banister:
prepare.

Unspeakable

The heart won't make its point.
Why not let you go out into the sun
where blossoms burst
and rush like Oxycontin?

The chickadee's precision in the pear
chastises my ear
to clearer witness than the cat-
piss stink these beauties flush

into the air. What
would I have you say
before getting in the car? What
would I have you do

to me? Do you see
the dogwood's sensitivity —
all these deep red crepe cups
candelabraed up

from Mrs. Abraham Malherbe's
lichen-lepered tree?
They skewer the sky
with the austere

ash-pointed spurs
of why they're here
no matter where they wish,
or if they wish, to be.

Friday Migraine

A bird, undeterred, tries to squeak
juice from April ice
as crocuses wince
behind black snow

though through the window
I wade into yellow
warmth as if into the aural form
vision has been tunneling toward —

tigered lemon flutes
trembling acetylene
and, past the nauseated pain,
Easter, blistering.

Optimism

I made a fascinating box. Then I broke
some boxes down. I smashed them
into boxed juice. Then I pulled over at the Ocean
Hall to see what monster might rise up within

its watery walls. Of course, it would be
the sea dragon oscillating galleon sails
delicate as scallion skins
through cylinders of glycerin.

Of course such a wonder is always off to war
with the darkness that surrounds
even aquariums; that grays in pain and says,
This is going to keep happening.

Yes, death will make the poem end.
But we'll drive on, listening to unloosed color
pencils roll out of plastic grilles, not unlike gills,
into crummy holes waggling seatbelt buckles

which I'll vacuum one day when
I'm truly old, and the sea dragons, then
the drawings of sea dragons, have sailed
back into their stalls.

Catch-All

Mother Dear, never apologize for nettles
I yanked in fury
from Lottie Shoop's side yard —

they stung me into seeing
fairy mosses lily pad
her middened juniper;

the quivering gobble of her chin,
teacup clicking dentures as she sprang
up into her wattled hut
and broke a rib

of aloe vera —
gel belling the top of that claw goblet.

It didn't cool the sting, and yet, noticing
sunshine thumbing plums in a string
catch-all

I was already well.

A Sorrow

You'll never hear my grandmother say *Yarrow* —
not the warble of émigré ecstasy escaping into a field of yellow
eggs-and-butter in her *Yare*;

nor the gruff kapow, like the hoof of a calf, of *row* —
the velvet toe of her top lip putting its foot down
on her bottom one, ending all discussion.

After Ashbery's Last Reading

for Olivia

Sky blushes upward like Whiffenpoofs or shirred
eggs weeping the gold-leafed hair of Venetian friars
as I accumulate Italy through texts: you craning to sip
espresso on the Ponte Vecchio in last season's City
Pedal Pushers, your neck's *meanwhile* eliding
eight years' sorrow as this sky sieves cream off plums
like some Master rouging bottoms in a hammam
or girls troubling over which clouds to call horsetails.
Rome, Amsterdam, and God filter through a pastor's
meme: Shia LaBoeuf rawring JUST DO IT, illuminating
His Most Holy Name on the pearl ceiling of all
we're capable of feeling here, in the latest Millennium
of cirrus wiggling rum-warm, orange-foiled bellies
across gaps in the Brutalist carpark as I round and brake,
round and brake down seven levels into New Haven.

Kumquat

A kumquat bush crouches in the sedge
            at playground's edge
            and I stand in the sand

mashing one of its persimmon thumbs
            till oil prickles perfume
            pills on its wax skin.

If I bite into this thin bright hide's
            sweet zest no marmalade
            can pickle or preserve

until the fruit itself squirts acid over
            those segments like
            an orange's in miniature

yet sourer than a lemon's for
            pretending not to be
            and cankered by

tiny twisted pits, aborted kindnesses
            one might call specks
            in a neighbor's eye

might I be able to swallow this
            fruit of spite?
            Might I like it?

Putting One On at Maxim's

One of those afternoons with Élan and his South Beach tan
In a floor-length coyote coat and matching tam
Driving through the roadblock by Cabrini Green
To Jetro Cash & Carry restaurant depot
Where we watched a man buy ten cases of glass Cokes
And a skinned goat over his shoulder like an Isaac.
I resolved to fill the tarnished pewter bowls with pub mix,
Use the private john with its dual Tender Vittles bowl,
Smile thankfully at Otto and Laura in the drink well;
To smile smile smile as the Édith Piaf impersonator tinkled
Unheard beneath the cocktail roar that was my glory.
There are worse fates than squeezing into a red velvet
Cabaret banquette to overhear through bulk-wine tang
She knows how to program the shit out of an event.
I worried over the pancake-pink walls of the antique
Powder room, its peculiar stink of unlaundered ruffles
Amid the banter hearing myself repeat the one about Lennon —
Here's where he said, "The Beatles are bigger than Jesus"
And public fury forced a hastily called press conference —
To a Facebook friend I'd brought in as a panelist
Who observed my crowfooted sparkle with grave pity
Wondering what kind of Batshit Betty would host salons
In a precise replica of Maxim's Paris in the basement

Of a Gold Coast condominium while elsewhere in the city
Nurses fed her husband a cocktail of Thalidomide
And her baby daughters bawled in the arms of a Serbian
Ex-swimsuit model paid overtime to hush them when
Just then Élan crowed through the Beaux Arts mahogany,
Alright, tell the guys to kill the houselights, Beautiful.

Grand Central

From the Russian blue dome inlaid
with constellations I float up through
the underground eateries' tile glow

and cab it from Park Avenue
fifteen years since Claudia auctioned
one of Lois's bronze cows at Cipriani's.

It's all still here, ochre and marmoreal,
cathedrals soaring through creosote,
inwardly fired, brooding jewels,

retail-grown calcite and tourmaline,
distilled into apothecaries, boutiques
for every tinct of tea tree oil

I once bought believing
the cure for every ill curatorial.

One World Trade

The rack of whale ribs flung:

gargantuan iron
toothpicks and gauze

optimism swaddling the site.

Then the warp-angled platinum
tower rising to a height

so defiant it conjures a comic book
Apocalypse, clouds row-

ing swiftly past as if all
of us below were riding it; while

atop the awning, an African
worker turns the O

in WORLD to polish it.

Dog Bites

Will you play with The Beast like a sparrow
And put him on a leash for your girls?
God (Job 41:5)

1.

Within high stone walls
we picnic above a giant cypress bole,
branches thrown down in stilled celestial
fury, as our girls twirl
downhill in their long dresses
to beatbox on the fountain shell.

Complete wellbeing aches
at the horizon, civilized sun hazing
high grasses, and a Pomeranian's even mane
wends its aura between unblown dandelions
as Fiona runs to pet
the nasty unleashed bitch.

2.

The next day ("Czarina"'s rabies certificate received)
we tear down the fence in the name of neighboring.
Husbands haul latticed flats and lay them down
not quite as gently as unwanted thoughts
that enter the mind in contemplative prayer;
as the line between us disappears,
our yard becomes their yard, theirs ours.
The dogwood in our back corner now canopies
a shared plot to scatter grass seed over;
where soccer balls got stuck, their hostas
variegate our peonies. How close we are
to naming grace when we catch the trace of fur:
rabbit fluff bitten from a burrow the doc dug
over there, to keep a fence between her nest
and our dog, who, amidst our swelling souls,
has beheaded seven kits and strewn them out as prizes,
oblong side-eyes confirming them as bunnies,
even if, in my surprise, I tell the girls
(who can't know otherwise) they must be voles.

3.

The ceiling fan spars with little
Childrens' squeals
Amid droning air
Compressors well-manicured
Shrubs conceal.

(Shouldn't zeal, if real, combust
The clutter of our English
Tudor, turn over
Butter lettuce pots, burst
The fertilizer?)

Who quivers in a tremble
Where the fence stood between
Us and the Eitels'?

Who waits to hear
Freshets trickle?

Whose facets glint,
Infinite with evidence of all this
Epektasis, dynamic as
Job's whale

Or even The Crocodile
Who eats grass like a bull
Who drags the swamp like a rake
Who makes the ocean boil —

Who, so unsentimental, He
Or She hauls up the savage
And the good
So intermingled

We can only be still
And listen for
Our neighbors' call?

All Day We Drove

All day we drove, eleven hours, to the crux
where my childhood, and yours, and theirs crossed —
a Sleep Inn bedded between horse farms
in the blue hills of Lexington.

In the car park, snails, zebra-striped and pearled,
scooched tiny glam ottomans across a gulch
that skidded to a creek it seemed we'd visited,
before.

Each stretched its foot (also its neck) into flesh horns
that hauled it forward, through acres of thicket
in whose dense secrecy
more snails whorled dun to emerald.

Not antennae, but tentacles, the girls told me —
eyes straining, on mucousy stilts,
as far from their shells as they could reach.
What do we have to teach them, love? They see.

Summer Storm Prayer
Fairfield, TN

Bar the doors, lower the ropes,
close up the porch like an ark
and rock as the rain whitens farms,
squelching sawdust farmers were trying to burn.

Dare it to slash at the laths,
gush off both side-roofs and tear
the dogtrot's aluminum
as it spanks rotted sills to sorghum.

Let the long porch dim,
chairs wobble with nobody on them,
the sky above the pasture roil
like butter-and-cream corn.

Huptemugs

Fairfield, TN

There's a spirit in me that admits no weakness.
Is it the best of me or worst?
Cow daisies burn their stars into the stalled air of pastures.
No one else cares whether they'll last.

I shirk the sick and go out to pick flowers,
Bushels of the tough and prickly-legged,
Whichever I can pull out of the gulch,
And push them into thunder-pitchers.
An invalid in a peignoir pulls the covers over her head
In the high cherry bed great-grandmother had made
To match the chest of drawers.

Solitudes gather under the Beau D'Arc.
I ache for the meanness, the glorious meanness
That knocked croquet balls into its soft meal trunk,
To hear the thwack of that mallet,
To be it, as it cleanly cracks and lets the other ball be gone.

Acquisitive gall made my people call themselves victorious.
They thought they won the Mexican War, among others.
One ancestor drove his bayonet into the dirt when he returned —
This tree is what took root and bloomed,
Though Beau D'Arcs grow complex in illness.
Locusts have chewed its thatch to frets,
Its leaves fluted crisp, poxed yellowish, kissed by the worm.

Huptemugs believed that train rides to the capital to hear
Charlemagne singing Franz would cure the soul
(As venison is cured) against life's turmoil —
They couldn't tolerate complaints of the feet,
Corns and hammertoes, evidence of rot.

If generous you might have called us committed to transcendence,
Though who that fought her way into an opera box
Ever let the arias consign her to a fate of constant care?
There is a spirit in me that admits no weakness.
When it sings, the rest of me despairs.

The Tavern Parlour
Fairfield, TN

A giant step up into the dip —
the unavoidable tremble of cocktail tumblers
against bottles of bourbon and bitters
droning the spittoon.

All dim, unwoken, shut
as the Duchess'
(née Clare Singleton's)
dust-caked woodcut gramophone

as the frail jail of Limoges and miniature
saltshakers belling at my footfall
recalls country wenches
doing the quadrille

with speculators' sons, and Ben
the Tavern "houseboy," in canary pantaloons
wafting a fan sewn from the tails
of fifty peahens

to keep off the Luciferian flies.

Trees
Fairfield, TN

Having forced the stiff U.S. Mail flag up
and left the card crackling among cricket nymphs,
the wheel ruts' little rocks nibbling at my soles,
the cattle grate a memory, a lock installed
to forbid locals from riding donuts on the lawn
or chucking empties in the boondocks
from which fireflies still drowse into the grasp
like spirits, Eliza says, *like will-o'-the-wisp* —
all at once they sweep up from the grass:
hackberry, coffee, sweet gum, ash, and beech,
centuries of speechlessness pitched to a high,
unfiltered exactitude my praise stabs at
even as they fall back to papery, aromatic stars
and elephant ears fruited savagely as maces.

Our Twenties

The way the oat bran blurps
recalls the promises we made
with what we called our souls.

Each bubble like a shade in hell
fills with the steamy air
of what it wishes that it were

before pulling its lips apart
in a disconsolate *"Mwa"*
and melting back into the meal.

Why do you haunt me — you I
haven't missed and don't wish to see
even, especially, after I die?

The way you burst then swell
up from the very belch into which
you were just sucked appalls me.

Yet I realize it's not just you
(or you, or you, or you)
off-gassing hope with every pop —

but my own soul dying to
rematerialize into what it was
before the oat bran turns to glue.

Leaving Boston Again

When I woke out of my reverie

(thank you Jesus thank you Jesus thank you Jesus
the scans weren't worse and make my life
a testimony to pure consciousness)

the oaks that swerve up East Rock Park
announced their white-barked symmetries
against the winter-darkened marsh
with such insouciance

I believed not only all of this was real

but that the clouds'
lavender croissants of vole fluff
such   soft   smudged   smut

might heal

not just us but the whole deal,

this Connecticut, by Constable

II.

Anyway in Spring

The cancer comes back again in March. Walking through the quad's crenellated cloisters, observing sunshine single out the Victorian graves, the gargoyles, the cobblestones casting their circumspect romance, she recalls that other March, three years ago, when her husband was being recruited, before the cancer came back the last time. How instantly she'd fallen for New Haven, this little city true to its name. Then, how soon after he'd accepted the offer, the fantasy of welcome had been met by the insult of the bad blood tests, the pain in the knee, boot treads clomping bluntly on bleak sidewalks. Look but don't touch. You can't have this. Don't let down your guard.

✣ ✣ ✣

Then, in April, the cancer goes away again, and her husband is released from the hospital with a shrug from the Communist-bloc doc. "Who knows, maybe it was just a virus," he grins. "We love viruses!"

In their neighborhood, buttercups smear Connecticut creeksides, profligate acrylic squirts, and their daughters gather bushels to hold under her chin and ask, *do you like butter?* Then affirm, by the degree to which her ever-whiter skin reflects yellow: *oh ho ho, do you like butter!* Blossoms riot the earth because her husband has had cancer for eleven years, but is still alive. Unreasonably gleeful, she prays in her Prius outside Planet Fitness' purple Judgment Free Zone, facing into two skull-shaped speakers between the headrests of a Chevette whose window reads NO JOKE in Olde English scroll, seagulls missiling down onto the asphalt to fight over a whole baguette none can lift, praising Connecticut, where she lives with her husband, kids, and dogs, and

blond reeds scallop the canals, wuthering
slithers behind the strip malls.

✛ ✛ ✛

They've stopped going to the church where worship took place in a huge modern log cabin, dream catchers hung from the eaves, and quotes from Abraham Joshua Heschel and Maya Angelou were fingerpainted on the windows. There, the Christians were professors, scholars of church history, and flinty New Englanders who, even in severest grief, persisted; who understood that Christian triumphalism was ahistorical, if not diabolical. Sermons often meandered into the latest geopolitical crisis — Syria or Zika — and ginned up the same diffuse, self-righteous empathy she felt after gorging on her Facebook feed. Meanwhile, she craved the word Christ, sharpened at the end, as if to skewer her inner ear.

Now on Sunday afternoons they drive downtown to a church whose pastor and congregants ask God directly, "What are You doing *here?*" and are willing to hear an answer. They seem liberal because of their t-shirts and Adidas, and because they agree that Trump may well be the Antichrist. But unlike the other liberal churches they've attended since her husband's diagnosis, this one believes in evil. These Christians think injustice comes from Satan. She wonders what they think causes cancer.

After the diagnosis, they'd moved through Cancerland as if it were an iced Atlantis. The escalators pulled them up to the next level of glass balconies or spilled them down to the ground floor, where people milled, with their afflictions and aspirations, past Barbara's Bookstore and *Pulse,* the hospital gift shop, its silk scarves pulled into pastel knots at the corner of her vision. She knew every entryway and exit, particularly the Skybridge connecting the parking lot to the second floor. She often walked swiftly above Saint Clair Street, between the various shades of ice blue, with a wind about her (that was not her) that was something like an avenging angel. It forbade her from looking down, at that other, briefly radiant, romantic Chicago: the expensive city, those blocks between the beach and the Ritz where they'd fallen in love. In all that hospital glass — some clear, some tinted aquamarine, some frosted or mellowed with milk — there was a certain concept of transparency that it behooved her to believe in. As if being seen were akin to being cured.

✢ ✢ ✢

Recently the doctors have started saying her husband's disease has moved "beyond the end of knowledge," which makes her wonder what happens now to all she thought she knew, back then. She knew, for instance, the double revolving doors of Northwestern's Galter Pavilion, outside of which the taxis parked, and which reflected the wide white panes of the Affinia Chicago. She knew the west-facing windows of the oncology waiting room that looked out on great, grated heating turbines and beds of furiously sparkling manila gravel. She didn't know the first oncologist because they'd fired him after he cornered them in the exam room with his Zeus grin and drew a diagram of her husband's projected life span on a whiteboard. Five to seven years.

But she knew Dr. Berman as one might have known the radiantly sober ghost of Gershom Scholem. His parents had been sent to separate Nazi concentration camps, where they each assumed the other had died, only to run into each other

— literally, bowed head to bowed head — at the water spigot in the middle of an enormous relocation camp after the war. Dr. Berman and his twin sister were two of the world's foremost research oncologists, responsible for many of the drugs that now kept terminally ill patients alive indefinitely. He was *calm* — so calm, her husband joked, you could walk in with a hatchet in your head and he wouldn't flinch.

She knew to bring her husband a Chicken Caesar Wrap from *Panoply!* on the days he got infusions; to let him sit up in bed, firing off emails, even as Crystal administered the drip; not to call it "chemo"; not to panic if he broke out in hives; to simply mash the CALL button and watch Crystal gallop in with Benadryl, burbling all the while over her recent humanitarian trip to Africa and the fiancé who'd quit her a week before the wedding.

She knew for the first time when she was twenty-eight years old, and knew it frantically every time the number after the decimal point in the blood draw ticked down. She knew it the way one knows a stiffened lymph node, rolling it like a fetish bead under the thumb, as they drove home, Chicago's Disney-fied Xanadus (the Rock n' Roll McDonald's, Rainforest Café, Excalibur) looming up around them, their promises of pleasure as tasteless as helium, even as the Dan Ryan drew them down into its grip, and the city prickled up behind them like "the needles of the fretful porpentine." She knew it as if it were the only thing worth knowing. So what does she know now?

✛ ✛ ✛

"Sure, take a look — they're incredible," her friend, the novelist, says, without tilting her head up to look at the prize-winning orchids tendriling down from her father's bespoke birdcage greenhouse. "The little bitches."

Their laughter meanders through the sculpted paths, a nautilus of East Coast consciousness so well considered even the touches of disorder — pokeweed meandering around the sunken slate — acquire an aspect of deliberate élan. The dogwoods arch over full rhododendrons and spigots of salvia with such structured poise that following the path to the pool house feels like following a flute, only to be surprised by a peaked gate, angular crimson as the crown of a Chinese child emperor.

Yet, as often happens with her friend, they sit, drinking their seltzers, acknowledging the glory of the weather and their children, while their conversation nevertheless returns to Death. The fox with kits stalking the chipmunks behind the herbs. The alligator in the Guadeloupe. The threats, mainly human, to camping. ("A cozy family, what stupid sitting ducks!"

her friend slavers, imitating a murderer.) And, most especially, within themselves: that place, beyond the pale, within the garden; that place of clarifying terror, which they each have touched and tasted, and to which they hope never to return; yet whose existence (whose intoxicating, annihilating knowledge) is witnessed by the understanding, twisted as DNA, into each others' eyes.

Meanwhile, the children plop to the bottom of the narrow pool, like a slotted fountain in a Modern museum, their neon Doppler-radar swimsuits dignified by the clear tonic tinged by slate-grey granite quarried from Stony Creek. Then, from Criss-Cross Applesauce, they erupt into an event they call Bubble Catastrophe, the highest pitch of which matches the cry of ospreys overhead.

If earth can make me this glad, do I need God? she wonders while walking the dogs through Spring Glen, the cherries and the lilacs whooshing in the wind, whipped into cream, while the "Thrush's eggs look little low heavens." When with instant ferocity her joy turns back on her to ask, *Well then is this the life you're called to sacrifice?*

Dualities are mean, she thinks. If any living things could withstand the Imperishable Light, they're these. Anyway, in spring, even the unuttered, abject prayer is answered with

violets' blue wigs madcapping medians
under the ALTERNATIVE HEALING sign

forsythia burnishing
its bottlebrush

cherries and pears and plums
rummaging blush from
shimmying hinds.

✝ ✝ ✝

Dr. Berman had been sanguine about the idea of them getting pregnant. "There's no reason you shouldn't," he'd said, smiling sagaciously as if to imply that there were many reasons that they should.

It would require some medical intervention. Her husband, first of all, would have to preemptively bank sperm because the Rituxan-Velcade trial had been shown to mutate DNA. She'd have to go in for surgery, to remove a uterine septum, a piece of extra tissue that descended into her uterus like the cleavage in a Valentine heart and on which an egg couldn't implant. All of this was uneventful, except for the fact that the sperm bank was staffed by a single man named Conrad, a bored fifty-something with bleached hair and an angular, leathery face that suggested hard decades spent as a cocaine-addicted cabaret singer. She and her husband thought it likely that, in his boredom, he had inseminated Chicago with leagues of little Conrads.

Nevertheless, they put ten vials on ice. Each time they used one, their chances decreased by ten percent. After the first two tries, the doctor, an ironic young Russian woman, prescribed Clomid, a low-key fertility pill, and when they didn't get results, she had to shoot herself up every morning by squeezing an inch of belly fat and plunging in a needle full of high-octane hormones. It didn't hurt. Soon, the ultrasound showed four viable eggs. What would happen if they all got fertilized? They asked, and were told that, by a process called "selective reduction," the four would be reduced. It was the terminology, its clinical efficiency, that spooked them. "I wouldn't worry," Dr. Svetlana said, her pale face coming briefly into focus in the middle of her smudge of frizzed hair. "With intrauterine insemination it's unlikely that even one gets fertilized."

But they didn't have to worry: when they went in for the next ultrasound, there were two embryos, exactly.

✣ ✣ ✣

The morning sickness struck the day after she harvested the cilantro that had bushed up in the square-foot garden they'd planted before she got pregnant. A lady at work who barked at everyone and liked to be called the Culinary Czar instructed her to make it into cilantro pesto. On their honeymoon in Costa Rica blue Morpho butterflies had lifted up from a meadow of wild cilantro in a clearing in the rain forest. Now she threw up cilantro pesto all night long.

For the rest of her pregnancy, Chicago reeked. Every alley and aperture huffed its steaming stinks at her, specifically. Spiteful cat piss and aggressive onions. The odors of Albany Park, the zip code in which more languages were spoken than any other in America, no longer liked her. Humanity, it seemed, could not respect her sensitivities. "I'm just like a giant garlic sausage walking in the door, aren't I?" her husband asked when he noticed her shrinking from him.

By then, the Rituxan-Velcade had worked, and Dr. Berman thought her husband was going to be fine. Lots of people were getting long remissions, and for some the cancer hadn't come back at all. Plus, Dr. Berman said, if there was any time to have cancer, this was it. Every day a new miracle drug was being born.

✛ ✛ ✛

Oh twins, what a blessing! I always wanted twins! women at the gym (where the elderly Polish ladies lotioned themselves in the steam room, slapping up their breasts and bellies, glaring at anyone who opened the door and released the pent-up heat) would say when they asked and she told them. Though often people asked, *do twins run in your family?* And once, later in pregnancy, when all the lifeguards warily observed her elephant-head-sized belly, a stranger in the locker room took her in and quipped, as if affronted, *Natural or IVF?*

Though the word *blessing* wheedled, wormlike, in her ear, as it always had, all sanctimonious sound and little substance, she couldn't deny she felt it, even on the last month of bedrest, as she lay on the couch, doggedly plowing through a tome on the Russian Revolution while her husband stockpiled a Doomsday supply of soups in the deep-freeze. She felt it bearing forth, breaking her back, seizing her legs with Charlie Horses, parching her and keeping her awake, that which she had for so long forsaken or been forsaken by, maybe because there was no word for it, this blessed-in-forsakenness, which she'd been slow to receive, but, now, she knew, was nearly here.

It's rapture, a friend had said of having babies, a friend who shared her fascination with St. Teresa. *But you're not supposed to say so.*

✣ ✣ ✣

The first days after the girls were born, doped on the freak luck of two perfectly healthy twins, she and her husband watched the girls' faces unfurl between walls of glowing lambswool. Baby A mashed down her lids with the wide set of a little lizard, smiled at some idea of the bountiful, contorted her lips into sideways hoots, rooted for a drink, and drew back with a smack. Baby B smirked as she slept, her eyebrows jigging, as if witnessing some amazement behind her lids; then yawned, then stretched, then goat-whinnied her way into a different dream. They bounced them on the yoga ball and napped with the lamps on and ate from the supply of soups. Outside, it was frigid February. Snow sugared the roofs of the garages, and ice pastry-flaked the block of chain-linked yards opaled by a hidden sun.

The first time they left the house alone, they took a walk around the block, through the neighborhood that had been advertised before the housing crash as HOT! ALBANY! PARK! The tax attorney, the Lavenderia, the funeral parlor proclaimed their INCENTIVOS, their GRAVITAS in bolds, their perishable selves screaming into the freezing, bright air. It occurred to her how long it had been since they'd actually looked at each other. When she turned to her husband, his clear gaze filleted her. "Do the babies make you think more about the illness?" he asked.

The white sky, blank as blotter paper, absorbed bare branches like aneurysms of ink. "Yes," she said in a tone not entirely kind. "But it doesn't change the joy."

✥ ✥ ✥

When the girls were two months old, her husband's blood test showed a slight uptick in a certain, unpronounceable protein, an ominous but inconclusive sign. When they were five months, his knee blew up again, this time to the size of a cantaloupe. At the end of the summer — when Snorty Bird had started making her Snicklefritz face and Baby Buddha had invented a dance move called The Shaker — they learned that his hemoglobin was below ten. His knee showed signs of "extensive necrosis." The bone had died. The orthopedist audibly gaped at the MRI and said, "I've honestly never seen anything like that before."

She walked into the nursery and saw the girls' toys: those primary-colored shapes that mothers are always waving before a baby's face, contorting one's own face into a mask of delight to conjure their delight, which, for them, is an emotion inseparable from seeing. The building blocks, the mirrored books, Mr. Whoozit — each of their shapes shrank through her like charms shrieking through a cauldron.

✥ ✥ ✥

She knew the words to the hymn, "What Wondrous Love is This," though they had always come to her at the wrong times, as once, shortly after the diagnosis, when she noticed a peach pit on the grass outside of a church in Chicago being devoured by ants. *What wondrous love is this, O my soul, O my soul.* The words washed through her as she watched the ants clean the pit of its last fruit. *What wondrous love is this / That caused the Lord of bliss / To seethe these feasting millions through my soul.*

When the girls were eight months old, her husband was admitted to the fifteenth floor with an infernal swelling under his chin, ten out of ten on the pain scale. No one had a clue what it was, and he simmered in bed for days as the specialists crept in to inspect him. The view of the water, glowering beneath the towers, was breathtaking. She sat on the windowsill staring down until her breasts hardened into missiles, then went into the bathroom to pump. When she got back, Lake Michigan looked as little and immutable as a geode under glass. She was a soul peering down through a rip in Paradise, at the infinite spiraling toward damnation, contemplating falling through that scalding air without her husband — and with, *my God,* their babies.

First he got his bones scoured by three treatments of Thalidomide-spiked chemo. For one week every month, they pushed his IV around a rink of reflected light, little lucid rooms where doctors and nurses and interns and PAs administered infusions. The tubing, the syringes, all of that precision, negated the urge to feel. Instead, the transplant team gave out gift bags of purple CELEBRATE LIFE key chains and thermoses. Then they harvested his stem cells. The morning of the transplant, a chaplain performed an interfaith blessing. A tech dressed in a Hazmat suit rolled in a hibachi full of dry ice that held the vial of her husband's potential life. The tech unscrewed the container slowly, making a show of it as he unleashed the genie from its cowl of smoke. Then, to break the silence, the young nurse with the magenta streak in her hair shouted, "You'll have two birthdays to celebrate now!"

"Do you like this stuff?" her husband asks.

She's found him at home, sampling a gift bottle of Laphroaig. "Yeah, sure, I love it. It's like sucking at the very source of Scotland."

"It's like drinking from a dwarf's butt."

He's got the crazy light about him that he had in the beginning. Before cancer. When everything that he said startled her. He always appeared abruptly — just back from the gym, body flexed within his crisp, blue business shirt; at her office door, offering her an apple; walking into Coffee Expressions as she was walking out. His eyes were lit, sharply faceted, prismatic almost, shooting in multiple directions at once, catching her at angles she didn't expect to be seen from.

After work, they'd slip out of the offices separately and meet at the elevator of his high-rise, which sucked them up to the twenty-second floor like a gasp. The fear of being fired magnetized the view, those skyscrapers whose shapely differences they'd admired from the deck of the Chicago Architecture Tour. How some seemed to drip upward, or devour their own reflections, or aim for opaquery, concrete steamliners with portholes for windows.

Now here he is, in their kitchen, twelve years later, his eyes' glacial blue deepening as he raises his eyebrows suggestively and says, "I like this flexible work schedule." Alive.

✤ ✤ ✤

During the recruiting visit, they'd stopped to see an old colleague, a designer respected for his protean, Modern touch. By coincidence he'd recently moved to Connecticut, too, bought a white Bauhaus-style tower on the highest point in town, and begun a massive renovation. The whole time he was undergoing chemo for incurable brain cancer. Gin-frizzled, bone-thin, he led them through the hanging streaks of construction plastic, the unfinished dream, while snow filled the valley below — the river, the yards, the factories, the red granite gulleys of the towering rock that buffeted the swoops of the red-tailed hawks. An elaborate Japanese garden, designed by the wife of the man who built the tower, twisted around one side of the property, but, as they gazed at it, their friend said he planned to demolish it. "It's got to go," he said from beneath his oversized woodman's cap. His eyes gleamed within his translucent face, just as they always had when he'd unveiled a new design. Why was he so radiant? He was about to die. What did he believe?

Make it new.

✢ ✢ ✢

Modern artists often have the most Puritanical aesthetics, she thinks upon waking, in America at least, per William Carlos Williams and the exhausted tone of "Spring and All." She, meanwhile, has become the sort who occasionally feels the urge to praise even azaleas,

the scarlet smirch of them, Velvet
Christmases and salmony
carpeting blurring into miniature
bottlebrushes, the awfuller
the azalea color —
the Gatorade, the cauliflower —
the more they overpower her
with the joy of being heard.

✣ ✣ ✣

By the end of May, all signs of the cancer have, impossibly, left her
husband's bloodstream. They refuse to say so out loud, to inform
their mothers, or to offer thanks at church. Yet, her husband
is, in fact, well enough that they are able to fly, all four of them,
to Texas.

It's still spring there, too. Wildflowers spray the weeds
under the mesquites, and between the cacti the frayed blue
and orange edges of Indian paintbrush blur into fields where
kids feed. A band of ibex graze on the pasture above the Uncle
Mitchell's cedar, while Fern, the neighbors' miniature milk cow,
moons like a pet around their fire pit and putting green. After
watching the sun rise on the horses, their daughters pretend
to ride their shadows, and run barefoot to rub their noses, sun
haloing uncombed hair and manes as one. Then they all walk

out together to pick flowers, as she did when she was little, in Tennessee, soaking their sneakers with dew. The girls call the bright pale starbursts "highlighters" and seek the rare pink lipstick hue that stairsteps up a raggy stem like an orchid, until, in a clearing among crabby black cedars thorned like a fairytale lair, one girl finds one, delighting the other, who vaults downhill squealing onto steps of prickly pear and waving grasses dabbed with foam.

They walk and pick till the dew burns off into true heat, then traipse up into the deer blind and sit together in its cool dark vestibule. The girls tell them what Uncle Mitchell said the window was for — to watch, not hunt, for game — when just then a troupe of antelope, a horned male and three females, spring on all fours out of the brush into their rectangle. Instinctually they all jump up and rejoice at such a sighting. As if this is what a deer blind were actually for.

III.

The Reason

It was, I thought, my trick to staying sane
when I'd rather have been smithereens,
so guarded it like any fundamentalism
as if it were my ticket, if not to fame, to heaven.

Then, one day, a name (I can't remember which
illness like a fate) switched places with my reason
but instead of going instantly insane,
hidden dynamism sieved my brain in both directions.

Where facts unstuck autumn leaves blew in
gradients of sunshine, unreasoning
each elementary yellow, red, and brown
into shallows of the most enviable Mediterranean.

But this was the clear fall air of our own town.
It blew through the space where facts had been
with a lucidity that refused to drown them.
As if to finish knowing were also to be known.

Alphabet City

On the other side of Stuy Town, pronounced
Stoy! Tone! between glugs on a forty of OE
by the skater who was about to rape me,
we climbed a graffitied wall as if the projects were
a Babel you had to risk your feudal life to breach.
How many tongues have I beseeched explaining
who they were and who I was and why I'd go
inside an elevator sclerotic with White
Owl smoke and ride so far up into a fable
I couldn't tell a baby's squall from a suicide?
My panic button's eye had been gouged out.
I had to grope my way through corridors
shook with fuck music using only the blown
wires hanging from my sockets into the squalid
bedroom overlooking east New York,
all the little windows tarpatched into the dark
attempting to impart *how fearful and dizzy 'tis*
to cast one's eyes so low, and still I said:
There is a cliff ... Bring me to the very brim of it.
Did I fear finally for my life once confined?
Or wretched in despair forget how and shaking
my great affliction off fall back to the busted
mattress on the floor, its sprung spring rusted

to gouge a measurable inch in my innermost
thigh? Did I know I wouldn't die? Could I
have guessed how long I'd have to lie there
staring at the ceiling crack observing
myself my soul escape my skin sulfured
by the searchlight tower's Stalinist glow —
twenty-five years of, where did she go?
was it my fault? who were her clear gods?
did they cut off her ears that I might hear You?

Pain Prayer

I am not dead yet.

My bare feet scale
shiny pocked
blue volcanic
rocks the floods have salved
into familiar shale

and between the pale
sand stripes
a rock's black oil
crinkles at my heel.

Every dimple reveals
the universe within
these stones is sound.

Let me clench all pain
on to this line
and let it down
into that starry stone.

Let me draw a sunfish
out of the Absolute
alone.

Let foil freckles
muscle its middle
as fire flexes gases
through a star.

Let me grasp its fins'
prehistoric axes
till their transparent
spires splice

the aren't
from who You are.

On Finally Reading Jane Kenyon

Reverent lust twisted Don's beard —
"Jane's peonies" to him
may as well have been plums Keats
nibbled from Fanny Brawne's palm.

Shied not by him but by the dead
woman whose hazel shells
he still fumed to form
his mouth around, I hid from her spell

in his grizzled fizz and house —
objects plonked about like found
poems and a discarded monograph signed
To Don, a don, from Ezra Pound.

Our girls napped in the garret
nestled in dusty asparagus and eggplant
throw pillows sewn by Nanny,
Don's tart maiden aunt, and loons

dipped through the ponds' loose coins
as June's high light mismatched
blackberry leaves, vetch, and poison
ivy in a clearing of nuthatches

who sang of spouses without compare —
cleared, I see now, by Jane,
her lines' clean pine seasoned to burn
fast, and plainly her own.

Small Plates with Poets

I will not quarrel or cry out, nor call anyone Hitlerian
Nor label Merrill mandarin nor note the egg-sucking
Satisfaction of The Poetry Queen reading *People* magazine.
I'll eat my langoustine beheaded and chat about The Line
As the prize judge bends her tendons like a fawn.

I'll eat chorizo braised in maple figs without breaking
A bruised twig, or stoning anyone as an adulteress.
I won't despair at the rose-gold and certainly secular
Ponytail of my friend, her face contained as a cochineal beetle's,
Her mind too precise to entertain a feast beyond taste.

I'll let her perfumed embrace make of me a Memory Foam,
Sampling tapas because it must be good to cure
Salami the pinks of frescoes washed of saltpetre,
To nip cheese spears down to the wax and declare oneself
More a woman than a cheese-paring after dinner.

I won't allow small foods or medieval meats to sadden me
The way pleasure saddens Marxists and Puritans.
I'll wait donkeylike as a divot-eared mutt,
Birdshot near his spine and not a thought in his velveteen skull.
I'll smile like a fool, and pray for a crumb to fall.

The Problem of Influence

When I walk out with my soft dinner roll
and the clouds occur to me as edible ash blebs,
Guelphs and Ghibellines smushing big bellies
and some a-fibs over Lake Whitney
a weepiness reclaims me, thinking of the dead
I never met, or met but once, bumpered
by my shiny youth and/or a banquet table's prow
between me and their Endowed Chair.
I looted a few biographies back then, for facts
to fire off in essays or at dinner parties — fun.
Now I plow into them like Neruda plowed
his unrequited love, seeking that grove
where memory and grief and brief likeness
with a don who saw himself as a Victorian
spinster coalesce around a ponkan tree.
Remember how easily the ponkan rinds ripped off —
powdery as bums, butter buns, or pom poms,
or the plums behind us once we'd made it home
all the way uphill from Plum Tree Park? No,
that was another pal, the one who says mish-*mosh*
instead of mash. Now compline bells (actually
Carillonneurs who strike the bars with their hand-heels)
startle the bored sky with Harkness' filigree.
It's weird, genuinely, how High Street squinnies —
an itty-bitty contrapposto wag, almost a wave,
wishing, *I'm Aliiive.*

Tail of the Yak

I never said "serendipitous," yet maybe Gaylee
(as Annabel, my mother's green parrot, called her)
called me, too, from Silverdale's parapet
as from within a virgin spruce,
for I'd started rejoicing twice, first at bees
then again at bee bodies classified from plain
to iridescent tourmaline, and those
in shallow tart tins, painted as parakeets.
In the Berkeley boutique we had to pull a bell to see
each masterpiece rewind to its generating detail:
a mantle dressed in icons dwindled to a Mexican
Chess set, every piece made up in a mask,
the Queen vamping like a Kabuki ingénue;
a Gaudi cathedral of Mozartian figurines
(including the same blue-wigged boy in pantaloons
Gaylee's mother, Omi, kept at Casa Blanca)
worried toward the crux of each chrysanthemum,
and me into a wonder akin to idiocy
so that I left my bag behind, with money and ID,
to follow curios into tinier, more crimson courtyards
as one follows a sorrowful song into a child's
homesickness, or any appalling loss, until

at the middle, I came upon a single lemon
hung in jasmine and eucalyptus, and heard myself
telling the children, *listen,* telling them *rejoice*
even as I wept like a lemon being juiced,
fog tucking in to the many-throated succulents,
which would lift by afternoon onto the hills.

Dutch

They left dirty toilets.
Host Review

Well then, let me hereby skewer the grandiose
Ambitions of Eva (and Joost) of Voorburg, the Netherlands
To become Superhosts when in fact the vacuous
Art House glamour of their BoHo bakery bespoke
A cleanliness so absolute even the toilet scrubber's
Pop-art cactus erased one's gross
Presumption at having squatted on their canvas.

"I like boring things," a giant white Andy Warhol
Quote announced above an immaculate red fridge
flanked by multiethnic naked swimmers fluttering
European jewels in cerulean wallpaper.
"Her things were so beautiful," my daughter said,
"But in a way that made you hate yourself,"
Thereby summing up the sin of certain art.

Some women are Mary Magdalenes, some Marthas
And some atheists use shame as discipline;
The Dutch word *schoon* means both "beautiful" and "clean."
In a hyper-lucid photograph above the scarlet stove
A schooner named The Twister cleaved the sea
Before a provincial carnival in which a Brueghelian
World of pains whined as intricately as a *speelklok*.

And why does one never hear a child screaming in Dutch
Supermarkets? Downtown, hausfraus contemplated Paprika
Lays, and a cow pianola groaned above the dairy
Yet only our kids could be heard crying "Mommy!
Cookies! Tony Chocoloney's! Why can't we have them all?"
Meanwhile Eva biked a daughter dressed in olive
Hygge through the cobble center in a *bakfiets*.

I had no scarves of boiled wool with which to cowl
A nine-year-old to bicycle between canals in driving rain
Uncomplaining but for the small scowl natives save
For squalls. Nor did I empty the dryer "reservoir."
Thus my daughters had to wear Christmas
Pajamas on the 12:34 from the Hague to Utrecht,
Where we were dismissed from the silent car.

On the other hand we don't dress up as Zwart Piet,
Sinterklass' nationally adored blackface sidekick
Whom the Prime Minister defended saying:
"My friends in the Antilles are very happy
They don't have to paint their faces. When I play Zwart
Piet I am for days trying to get the stuff off my face."
Nevertheless my own face in photos has fallen

To resemble the medieval belltower called The Dom
In which we hugged our guts, then thundered the *toiletten*,
Frowning as we dropped our euro in the can. We ate, we slept,
We pooped, they screamed how bad it hurt to poop,
How much they had to poop and couldn't. We looked up poop
On Google Translate. It's *achterschip* or sometimes *kak*.
Other than *dank je* it was the only Dutch we had.

Saint's Novella

I saw a rose tree high as the cypresses
In a place Pomponius or Saturus had torn
Violets all over the grass

The rose tree was the brilliant, never-
Written book I ruined
My neck sniffing the attar of

The violets were the witty titles
That had flashed over my brain

Like insights lighting into the very
Heart of pain

Where I might have written Love

The New Nice

2020

Catastrophe closes us into the house.
What I thought an aimless brick suburban Tudor
becomes clear utterance. It says No
wherever I would've said Yes.

No longer must I be nice to anyone
except the people in this house.
Niceness, it is obvious to me now,
lets out what should be hemmed.

It mists lawns and portions of pavement.
It spends, and it spends, on acquaintances.
It pretends an open face, an "open
personality" (as a bad boss described mine once)

an invitation. What am I saying?
A sunny day, bicycling neighbor gangs, loud boys
playing not quite six feet away mean to
harass this house? That's not very nice.

But this is my property. I've decided
these daffodils and tulips are mine to keep or kill.
Perennials rage up every May along this edge —
an edge I would prefer you keep your doggy off.

I'm tired of speaking in Telephone Voice.
May-I-please-speak-to-so-and-so? No.
I'm closing the door now. It sticks.
But once it gives it locks with an important click.

Apologies to Borges

Then one day the earth shucked itself and quivered
clear animal.

The pain, the stiff awfulness of life, remained
but I walked through a spring wherein
every shape that could be named could mean.

The Elephant Ear unwhorled its clamshelled jade ...

Cam, the large gay dad from *Modern Family*,
poured matador duende into the *Lion King* ...

The double plum's ecstatic grail revealed its title
in "The Library of Babel"...

And, by way of Vindication, a chickadee existed
in the spruce as if to say:

Axaxaxas mlö. To speak is to fall
into tautology but today it's obvious

I mistook for nonsense the most elegant hope.

Tulip Tree

The goddess face
Carved of space
Can only be seen once
She's weeped half her magnificence
Into the grass.

Petals around her neck
(Fuchsia toucan beaks last week)
Seek neither worship nor respect
But merely to reflect
Pink witness its peak.

Trespassing with Tweens

After arguing, gasping up at the Great Blue
Herons flap into the cypresses, we hush into mosses
and fallen needles auburn as wood doves.

All around us the forbidden Water
District's lily pads flex their mirrored hides.

Now another clatters back from his wide hunter's glide,
brings in his wings' ungainly myth,
folds his fisherman legs and straightens the tremendous
S-beard of his neck.

His pterodactyl face, almost all beak,
focuses in a yellow twinge that wells into an eye;
a black stripe streaks into his crest's flung jot.

You hate how distracted I get, my incomprehensible flights.
But you comprehend this pair of herons
sitting down on their extravagances to feed their chicks.

And now you're shrieking at their clucks, their gullying barks.
For a heron parent has tilted his or her face
formally as a watering can toward a vase
fluffed by what we're certain is

                              (Look, Mommy, look

look look!)

                two smaller beaks and an opening.

Monks

I've met one named Pheonix Jiránek,
ringleted and effusing "contuition"
as gaily as a Franciscan in a boat
eating honeycakes with an angel.

Thus the Lord showed me both ways,
the austere and the hospitable, are good.

This morning I pray, make my food
honeycomb. Let me feed
on names caught out of solitude:
Cronius, Achilles, John the Dwarf.

Sweeten my awkwardness as I morph
into this weird, glad cloud of witnesses.

Let my shortcomings be laid
at my own door.

Notes

Epigraph and *The Poem*

The opening epigraph is an excerpt from "And I Was Alive," a poem by Osip Mandelstam, translated by my husband, Christian Wiman. "The Poem" makes reference to Nadezhda Mandelstam, author of *Hope Against Hope,* and, by extension, to her husband, the poet, Osip Mandelstam. Christian translated a book of Mandelstam's poems, *Stolen Air* (ecco, 2012), with Ilya Kaminsky.

Leaving Boston

Ibrutinib is a BTK inhibitor, a newer class of cancer drug.

Dog Bites

All italicized lines are adapted from *The Book of Job,* translated by Stephen Mitchell.

Epektasis is a concept first articulated by the 4th-century Christian mystic St. Gregory of Nyssa. The word is typically translated from Greek to mean the soul's "eternal straining toward God."

Summer Storm Prayer, Huptemugs, The Tavern Parlour, and *Trees*

The setting of these four poems is the Fairfield, TN tavern built in 1790 that is the author's family home and the main setting of *Holler: A Poet Among Patriots,* published by Unbound Edition Press in Fall 2023.

The word "Huptemugs" was reportedly in local use at the turn of the 20th century, among local African-Americans, to refer to "high-quality white people," though this is very likely a self-congratulatory white legend.

Leaving Boston Again
John Constable (1776 — 1837) was an English landscape painter. The Yale Center for British Art holds several of his "Cloud Study" paintings.

Anyway in Spring
In explaining her own distaste for Modernist libertinism, Marianne Moore said, "All my stinging legs stand out like the fretful porpentine when I am told that if I were cosmopolitan I'd like lewdness too."

"Thrush's eggs look little low heavens" is from Gerard Manley Hopkins' "Spring."

Alphabet City
Italicized lines are from Shakespeare's *King Lear*.

Tail of the Yak
Tail of the Yak was a Berkeley boutique opened in 1972, which sold rare and exquisite crafts from around the world. It permanently closed in 2023.

Apologies to Borges

Several phrases in this poem are borrowed from Jorge Luis Borges' short story "The Library of Babel," as translated by Andrew Hurley, including *"Axaxaxas mlö"* (the title, in the story, of a book written in a language no living person can read); "To speak is to fall into tautology"; and "the most elegant hope."

Small Plates with Poets

Matthew 12: 19 — 20: "He shall not strive, nor cry; neither shall any man hear his voice in the streets. A bruised reed shall he not break, and smoking flax shall he not quench, till he send forth judgment unto victory."

From Shakespeare's *King Henry IV, Part 2, Act III, Scene 2,* Falstaff: "I do remember him at Clement's Inn like a man made after supper of a cheese-paring: when a' was naked, he was, for all the world, like a forked radish, with a head fantastically carved upon it with a knife."

Acknowledgements

My gratitude to the editors and readers of the publications
in which these poems previously appeared, sometimes in
slightly different form: *The Atlantic, Commonweal, Literary
Imagination, The New Yorker, Orion, Ploughshares, Poetry,
Subtropics,*and *The Yale Review, Together in a Sudden
Strangeness* (Knopf), *Gracious: Contemporary Poems in the
Twenty-First Century South* (Texas Tech University Press),
and *Resistance, Rebellion, Life* (Knopf).

Deepest thanks to Peter Campion, Patrick Davis, and
Atsuro Riley for their vision and their thoughtfulness; and to
the Association of Literary Scholars Critics and Writers for
their generosity.

To the first readers of the book, who helped it find its form
— Katherine Larson, Emily Warn, Averill Curdy Murr, Nate
Klug, and Simone Di Piero   I'm so thankful for your keen eyes
and ears, and for your friendship. And to Naeem Murr, Alison
and Adam Eitel, Ilya Kaminsky, Penelope Pelizzon, Peter Cole,
Adina Hoffman, Amy Herzog, Sam Gold, Richard Deming, Nancy
Kuhl, Samantha Thornhill, Lizzy Donius, Ken McGill, and
Chloe and Matt Shaw — thank you for bestowing on me and on
this book, time and again, the Falstaffian gift of "more life."

To my children, Fiona and Eliza; my mother, Gayle; and
my life's friend, Olivia, thank you for "dealing out that being
indoors each one dwells." And to my first first reader, my partner,
my love, Christian: May I hold your hand?

About the Author

Danielle Chapman is a poet, nonfiction writer, and lecturer in English at Yale University. Her previous collection of poems, *Delinquent Palaces,* was published by Northwestern University Press in 2015, and her memoir, *Holler: A Poet Among Patriots,* was released by Unbound Edition Press in 2023. Her poems have appeared widely, including in *The New Yorker, The Atlantic, The Nation,* and *Poetry,* and she was the the winner of the 2022 Stephen J. Meringoff Prize in Poetry, awarded by the Association of Literary Scholars, Critics and Writers. She has written essays and reviews for *The Oxford American, The Yale Review, Commonweal, The New York Times Book Review,* and elsewhere. For several years, Chapman served as the Director of Literary Arts and Events for the City of Chicago, and she was also an editor at *Poetry* Magazine and the Poetry Foundation. She currently teaches Shakespeare and creative writing, and lives in Hamden, Connecticut with her husband, Christian Wiman, and their twin daughters, Fiona and Eliza.

About the Type and Paper

Designed by Malou Verlomme of the Monotype Studio, Macklin is an elegant, high-contrast typeface. It has been designed purposely for more emotional appeal.

The concept for Macklin began with research on historical material from Britain and Europe dating to the beginning of the 19th century, specifically the work of Vincent Figgins. Verlomme pays respect to Figgins's work with Macklin, but pushes the family to a more contemporary place.

This book is printed on natural Rolland Enviro Book stock. The paper is 100 percent post-consumer sustainable fiber content and is FSC-certified.

Boxed Juice was designed by Eleanor Safe and Joseph Floresca.

Unbound Edition Press champions honest, original voices.
Committed to the power of writers who explore and illuminate
the contemporary human condition, we publish collections of poetry,
short fiction, and essays. Our publisher and editorial team aim
to identify, develop, and defend authors who create thoughtfully
challenging work which may not find a home with mainstream
publishers. We are guided by a mission to respect and elevate
emerging, under-appreciated, and marginalized authors, with
a strong commitment to advancing LGBTQ+ and BIPOC voices.
We are honored to make meaningful contributions to the literary arts
by publishing their work.

unboundedition.com